UNIVERSITY OF NORTH CAROLINA
STUDIES IN THE ROMANCE LANGUAGES
AND LITERATURES

WORDS AND DESCRIPTIVE TERMS FOR 'WOMAN' AND 'GIRL' IN FRENCH AND PROVENÇAL AND BORDER DIALECTS

GEORGE C. S. ADAMS

CHAPEL HILL

1949

UNIVERSITY OF NORTH CAROLINA
STUDIES IN THE ROMANCE LANGUAGES
AND LITERATURES

WORDS AND DESCRIPTIVE TERMS FOR 'WOMAN' AND 'GIRL' IN FRENCH AND PROVENÇAL AND BORDER DIALECTS

GEORGE C. S. ADAMS

CHAPEL HILL

1949

Copyright, 1949
The University of North Carolina

PREFACE

The numbers immediately following dialect and patois terms are the numbers under which von Wartburg has listed lexicographical items in his Bibliographie des Dictionnaires Patois (Paris, 1934).

When the Atlas Linguistique de la France has been used, points on the maps have been designated under the correct number preceded by a small n to avoid any confusion between this numbering and that of the Wartburg items. In instances where terms from the ALF were used, the name of the departement in parentheses follows the term in the main body of the text.

The place of origin of each term is explained in footnotes in the majority of cases—usually the name of a town followed by the name of the département in parentheses. In cases where terms were of a more general origin the name of the region (old province, canton, etc.) has been indicated.

To avoid the necessity of having the printer use a number of costly symbols, diacritical marks have been described and explained in footnotes whenever in the source there existed more than one such mark in connection with a single letter of a term, whenever a mark was used in connection with a letter rarely so marked, and whenever some phonetic symbol, echo vowel, or orthographic device was used.

Abbreviations which are not self-explanatory are those used by Wartburg and those found in the third edition of Meyer-Lübke's Romanisches etymologisches Wörterbuch (Heidelberg, 1935). In order to conserve space Wartburg's key to his own bibliography has been used instead of complete bibliographical references. The exact title of each book referred to can be found by consulting his work. For the same reason miscellaneous items not found in Wartburg's bibliography and consulted rarely for this study are cited by title only in the footnotes. Following the practice of the Linguistic Society of America, I have used italics only for linguistic terms cited or discussed, and have referred to volume and page numbers in the notes using Roman numerals for the volume numbers followed by a period and then by the page number. Other than first editions are cited in the bibliography by raised numerals immediately following the titles.

I should like to express my appreciation to Dr. Urban T. Holmes, Jr., Professor of Romance Philology in the University of North Carolina, who suggested to me the subject of the present study. Without his constant advice and encouragement it could not have been completed. Others I should like to thank are Dr. Robert W. Linker, of the University of

North Carolina, for useful editorial suggestions, Miss Rosalyn Gardiner for help in editing and arranging material, and Mr. Fred J. Allred for his research assistance during the early stages of this work.

CHAPEL HILL, N. C.
    February, 1949

TABLE OF CONTENTS

Preface	iii
Introduction	vii
I. Bringue	1
II. Cabasse, Cavasson	3
III. Chen-ma	4
IV. Commere	5
V. Dame	6
VI. Other Terms Built on Domina and Terms Built on Dominicella	9
VII. Femella	15
VIII. Femme	19
IX. Fille and Fillette	25
X. Gahe, Gage, Gagui, Gaja	29
XI. Garce, Gache, Gechotte	30
XII. Gore	33
XIII. Gouge	34
XIV. Gouine	36
XV. Guenipe	37
XVI. Guinche	38
XVII. Hor	39
XVIII. Jacasse	40
XIX. Jasasse, Jasress	41
XX. Moller	42
XXI. Pucelle	43
XXII. Pute, Putain	44
XXIII. Salope	46
XXIV. Terms on the Same Stem as Femme	47
XXV. Terms Derived from Filia	50
XXVI. Terms Derived from *Bacassa, *Bagassa, Baches	52
XXVII. Miscellany	59
XXVIII. Conclusion	90
Bibliography	91

INTRODUCTION

In recent years there has been an increasing interest in the intensive study of dialects and patois. Von Wartburg's critical bibliography of dialect and patois lexicographical items has served as a key reference work for the present study.

The following work is an attempt to bring together formations on the Classical Latin *femina, domina,* and a few kindred words in the regional and border dialects of France. A second aim is the consideration of descriptive terms for *woman* and *girl* in the same territory. The general purpose in both cases is to note the variation in form and meaning current, in the speech of the locales studied, through the observation of a small number of related word groups.

In addition to derivatives from Latin words considered the study is limited to descriptive terms, diminutives, and augmentatives. The descriptive terms are of several types, some of which express pejorative concepts, derision, derogatory epithets, and others express compliments or endearment. Many are terms applied to women only by extension of meaning. All locutions and all purely *nomina agentis* that possess no qualifying attributes have been excluded.

CHAPTER I

BRINGUE

The word *bringue* has two meanings of about equal frequency and importance. The first is that of 'unruly horse' and the second 'badly built woman', the locution *en bringues* 'in pieces, in bits, in disorder', being often used.[1] Gamillscheg defines it as 'piece, fragment, morsel', remarking that it is of the 18th Cent., existing in Norman and in Poitevin.[2] He refers to another authority who claims that *bringue* is a nasalized form of Mod. Fr. *brique* 'brick', which exists as *brico, brigo* today in Fr. Switzerland and Mod. Prov. with derivative forms in Languedoc and Rouergue: *brigaut* and *brocotte*.[3] He also cites the Norm. *brique* from the Dutch *brik*, and the expressions *bringue de femme* and *bringue de cheval*, used contemptuously.[4] In Norm., Dauph., and Saintongeais, *bringue* means 'frivolous-minded, careless woman', often used contemptuously. In Lyonnais it means 'thin, slender girl'; in Anjou, 'bad horse, bad woman'. *Bringuer* appears frequently in other dialects meaning 'to leap down', Limousin *bringa* 'to dance, hop'. Gamillscheg traces it back to the Frankish *springan, from the Old Saxon, meaning 'to leap', coming through Old Fr. *espringuier*, and suggests a connection with Fr. *brin*, as in *brin d'homme* and the Angevin *brin de fille*.[5] Meyer-Lübke gives the etymon as the Gaulish *brinos* 'rod, whip', the same one which he gives for *brin* 'sprig, slip, stalk', but says that the *-nge* is unexplained.[6] Bloch gives *bringue* 'badly made horse' as attested in 1751; used in speaking of a woman in 1808—*en bringues* being common in patois, and states that the etymology is unknown.[7] Cotgrave, strangely enough, gives *bringue* as a masc. noun meaning 'a drinking (to)'.[8]

In the dictionaries examined this *bringue* occurs (with the meaning 'badly built woman', unless otherwise noted): *bringue* 2, 143, 356, 398, 486, 552, 800,[9] *bringue* 789,[10] *bringue (brĕk)* 560,[11] *bringo* 789, 991,[12] 987, *brĕg* 204 'large badly proportioned woman of little intelligence', *brĕga* 978,

[1] M. P. E. Littré, Dictionnaire de la langue française 2.1897.
[2] E. Gamillscheg, Etymologisches Wörterbuch der französischen Sprache 149.
[3] See note 2.
[4] See note 2.
[5] See note 2.
[6] REW 1304, FEW 1.530.
[7] O. Bloch, Dictionnaire étymologique de la langue française 1.101.
[8] R. Cotgrave, A Dictionarie of the French and English Tongues.
[9] Defined as 'a girl or woman of great height who has the manner of a man'.
[10] Forézien.
[11] Messin at Vigy; L'Isle at Maizières and Verny; Pays-Haut at Amanvillers and Gorze; Nied at Frécourt, Sorbey, and Rémilly. Zeliqzon 560 gives four meanings:

1

'awkward girl, shameless'.[13] Mod. Fr. *bringue*[14] occurs in Paris argot, meaning 'large ridiculous woman'; in Bessin patois, 'awkward, clumsy woman'; Jublains (Mayenne, Blois), 'term of scorn in regard to women'; at Nantes, 'woman built like a lath or prop for a vine', i.e., 'thin'; in Angevin, 'awkward or wicked woman or girl'; in Fr. Flanders, 'girl of evil life'; in Artois dialect, 'street-walker, ungainly woman'; in Poitevin dialect and in Bas-Gâtinais dialect 356, 'a lean woman of bad appearance or poor figure'; in dialects of the Centre of France 398, 'a large woman with a poor figure'; at Varennes, 'badly built woman, abashed woman'; at Yonne, 'insult among women, sterile woman'; at Clairvaux, 'a woman careless in her dress, awkward, without grace'; at Ramerupt (Aube) 486, 'large clumsy girl'; in Lorraine, 'a girl or woman of great height'; in Moselle region 560, 'very large woman, old and talkative woman, dissolute woman'; at Doubs, 'crazy, shameless woman'; at Lyon 748, 'giddy, thoughtless girl of poor bearing or carriage; tall and awkward girl'; at Clermont-Ferrand, 'large, poorly-built woman'. In Gaumet patois 552, *brinque* means 'woman of lax morals'; in Bouillon, 'woman without honor'. Gaston Paris states that *grande bringue* means 'large, badly-built girl'.[15] At St. Pol *brĕg* means 'large, badly-built woman of very little intelligence'. In Gr. Combes *brig* means 'girl of evil life'. In Demuin *brenque* means 'badly-built woman, badly dressed'. In Savoy, *bringa* is a 'person without character that one can't depend on'; in Limousin, 'heedless girl'; in Perigord, 'girl who gads about, streetwalker'. In Crémine (Jura béarnois), *brĕga* means 'large woman'; at Vinzelles (Puy-de-Dome), *brĕga* has the sense of 'clumsy, awkward girl'. At Broye-les-Pesmes (Haute-Saône), *vieille bringue* is an 'aged woman who speaks at random, or a cow'. In Bas-Limousin (Corrèze), *bringo* means 'heedless girl'. With a different initial sound in Angevin speech and in that of Loches (Indre-et-Loire), *dringue* 'large badly-built or wicked person (said also of the beasts)', from which came the Angevin *dringuet*, 'alive, alert, careful of one's person'. In Aude patois *bringue* has the meaning 'tall thin girl'; in Picardie, 'large badly-built girl'.[16] At 667 *bringuer* and *bringeuse* mean 'chicaneur'.[17]

---

(1) 'bad horse', (2) 'very tall woman', (3) 'old woman who talks at random', (4) 'dissolute woman'.

[12] According to Béronie 991 this has also the meaning of 'large awkward girl who does nothing but romp and skip about'.

[13] The final *a* here tends slightly towards an *o*.

[14] This and the remaining items in this section (except when a lexical number is given) were taken from FEW 1.530.

[15] FEW 1.531; Wartburg states that it is unclear to him how *bringuenaudée* 'woman of evil life, nag (horse)' is retained as an etymon for *grande bringue* when *bringue* is the precise one, and gives as a probable reason the article *Bringuenel* 'nigaud' by G. Paris in Romania 33.559.

[16] FEW 1.530.

[17] Noun and adj.

CHAPTER II

CABASSE, CAVASSON

Cabasse 330, or *cavasson* 703, is a name which when applied to a woman is always taken in a pejorative sense, but which when applied to a child means that the infant is talkative. It may be derived from the crossing of *(*cur*)*curbacea* 'squash' with Arabic *qar'ae* 'gourd',[1] though another etymon has been suggested.[2] *Cabasse* 330 may have undergone an evolution of meaning as follows: 'squash-head', 'soft-head', 'empty-head', 'prattling, talkative'. That it comes from *cavus*[3] is unlikely. *Cavasson* 703[4] is said of a woman whose dress is always soiled. It may be an augmentative from *cabasse* possibly deriving its significance directly from the pejorative meaning of the latter, referring to the unattractiveness of the woman as a whole, not merely to her empty-headedness.

[1] Gam. 172; ZRP 28.149.
[2] Littré. op. cit. 1.445 gives *cabasser* 'to babble, prattle' *cabas* Celt. *cab* -Lat. *-acius, -aceus*, or Lat. adj. *capax* 'large, roomy, spacious'. This is very unlikely.
[3] Sainéan, ZRP 30.569.
[4] At Annecy in arr. of Annecy.

Chapter III
CHEN-MA

Chên-mâ 703, 's. m. et f.; literal: qui sent mal; se dit principalement d'une femme qui affecte des aires de grandeur au-dessus de sa condition'.[1] Other occurrences are: *chem* 1044 and *chema* 1044. The derivation of these is uncertain. There may have been some influence from *femo* 1044. Possibly the term could have been derived from *canis malus*, or it might even have been formed recently from *sent mal* 'male olet'.

[1] Thônes (H.-Savoie), A. Constantin and J. Désormaux in 703.

CHAPTER IV

COMMERE

Commère is derived from the Ecclesiastical Latin *commāter*[1] 'godmother' and is used in that sense as well as for the second mother of a child.[2] Its original meaning is little used today in the French and Provençal dialects, in some of which it has the significance of 'midwife, woman in childbed'.[3] In Old Fr. it had the meaning of 'godmother'.[4] The word has a number of meanings today: 'term of friendship used by people who see each other often, talkative and evil woman'.[5] Littré cites a number of dialect forms: *coumère* (Saintonge) (Berry), *comaire* (Prov.).[6] Among other such forms are: *comér* 38, *kimér* 105 'godmother, young girl, curious and talkative woman', *kimérress* 105, *commere* 164 'gossipy woman or girl', *comère* 233, *coumère* 356, *coummere* 419,[7] *coumèro* 987, *coumaire* 789,[8] *coumai* 789,[9] *counmaire* 789,[10] *comare* 789,[11] *comay* 789.[12]

[1] Bloch 1.162, REW 2082.
[2] Bloch loc. cit.
[3] See note 2.
[4] F. Godefroy, Dictionnaire de l'ancienne langue française 9.133. He cites: 'A Crestyène, me *coumere*' (1284, Test. de Jeh. Baboe, A. Tournai).
[5] Littré, op. cit. 1.684-5.
[6] See note 5.
[7] Canton of Varennes-sur-Allier (Allier).
[8] Gascon.
[9] See note 8.
[10] Rouergue.
[11] Dauphinois.
[12] Old Prov.

Chapter V

DAME

Dame is derived from C. L. *domina* 'mistress of the house, lady' through V. L. *domna*.¹ The form *dame* shows the reduction of the vowel (*o* to *a*), an infrequent but not rare occurrence in Old Fr. when a word is in an habitually unaccented position before another word as in a title, address, or salutation, and when the *o* precedes a Sonorlaut.² In the Middle Ages this was a title given to the wife of a noble as distinguished from that of a bourgeois, being thus restricted to women of noble blood till the beginning of the 17th Cent., when it took on its general current use as a title applied to any married woman.³ There still exist a number of specialized meanings. That of the Middle Ages is of feudal origin as is *dominus*, which in Gallo-Roman territory signified 'lord, master of a fief' during the Merovingian and Carolingian periods. Besides *dame* Old Fr. had the forms *dan(s)* and *dam*, Old Prov. *don(s)*. The Mod. Prov. forms are generally *domna*, *dona*, and *dompna*. 'Woman, female, wife, mistress'⁴ are the general meanings. In the following list of occurrences in the dialects and patois the meanings have been indicated only when they differ from the ordinary: *damm* 38, *dam* 105, 217 'mother, pregnant woman', 560,⁵ 892, 627 'mother', *dame*,⁶ 145, 208, 334, 398, 411, 743, 745, 989, 1034, 1047, *danme* 198, 478,⁷ *dãm* 204,⁸ *dam* 204,⁹ *dèãm* 204,¹⁰ *dãm* 209, *dem* 320, 594, 586, *denna* 373, 742, 789,¹¹ 805,¹² *dainme* 453, *dem* 560, 581,¹³ *dème* 560,¹⁴ *dem'* 570, *dēm*

---

¹ REW 2733; G. Körting, Lateinisch-romanisches Wörterbuche 3.3075; Bloch 1.199; F. C. Diez, Etymologisches Wörterbuch der romanischen Sprache 5.559; Littré 2.948; Gam. 321; Godefroy 2.414: *dame* 'mother-in-law, step-mother'.
² FEW Lieferung 13.126; AGI 3.330; U. T. Holmes in Language 11.231–7.
³ FEW lief. 13.124.
⁴ 'Mistress' is equivalent to *maîtresse*.
⁵ Fentsch patois at Fontoy; Vosgien patois at Gondrexange, Lorquin, and Réchicourt.
⁶ This form is cited by J. Brütting, Das Bauern-Französisch in Dancourts Lustspielen (peasant vocab. near Paris); at Paris and at Namur, see FEW Lief. 13.124.
⁷ Possesse.
⁸ In general usage. Here *a* bears a grave accent in source consulted.
⁹ In banlieu; as printed in its source *a* tends toward *e*.
¹⁰ In banlieu. In source consulted *a* bears a grave accent.
¹¹ Forezien.
¹² At Forez.
¹³ In its source *e* is printed with a small arc directly under it opening toward the right.
¹⁴ In general usage.

590,¹⁵ děm 590,¹⁶ de:m 594, dăm 590, donna 601, 786, 789,¹⁷ 866, 901, 1028 'femme', děm 604, dan-ne 614, danne 620, dan 629 'mother', damma 647, donna 647 'mother',¹⁸ domna 647, 789,¹⁹ dŏna 669,²⁰ dona 675,²¹ dóna 675 'mother', donne 702 'mother-in-law', donne 702 'mother of the family',²² dama 751,²³ damă 703,²⁴ dâma 721, dama,²⁵ 759, 764, 767, dana 763 'femme de petit peuple', 775, 789,²⁶ damo,²⁷ 788, 805, 815, 838, 848, 890, 921, 1008, 1009, 1023, dono,²⁸ 789,²⁹ 848,³⁰ 895, 896, 917, 1022, donno,³¹ 858 'grandmother', 789,³² 805,³³ douogno 789 'old woman, ugly woman',³⁴ duegno 789 'old woman, ugly woman',³⁵ dauno 789,³⁶ 1026, daune,³⁷ 789,³⁸ doana 789,³⁹ dompna 789,⁴⁰ damna 866, done 902,⁴¹ dàma 978,⁴² dâmo 987, dāmo 991,⁴³

¹⁵ In its source e is printed with a grave accent.
¹⁶ A as in note 10.
¹⁷ Old Prov.
¹⁸ Swiss. This term has the regular meaning also.
¹⁹ F. Hemmann, Consonantismus des Gascognischen bis zum Ende des dreizehnten Jahrhunderts. Old Prov.
²⁰ In its source o bears a dot under it and an acute accent over it; the word is obsolescent.
²¹ O as in note 20.
²² In its source e is printed as the Fr. phonetic symbol for mute e. This term has the regular meanings also and is used by children.
²³ This was cited with a long mark under the a.
²⁴ Thônes in the arr. of Annecy.
²⁵ Philipon, Dialects Bressan, in Rev. de phil. fr. et de lit. 1.107–19.
²⁶ Forézien.
²⁷ FEW Lief. 13.124, at Cahors this has the special meaning of 'female ghost'.
²⁸ FEW supra, Toulouse.
²⁹ Alpes dial.
³⁰ Pallas 848 cites this as meaning 'femme', damo from the same region having the regular meaning of 'dame'.
³¹ In Briançonnais (H.-Alpes) this has the special meaning here listed.
³² Alpes dial.
³³ Briançonnais.
³⁴ Rouergat dial. (Dép't. of Aveyron).
³⁵ See note 34.
³⁶ Gascon dial.
³⁷ Cited by Hemmann op. cit., also in use in arr. of Oloron (Basses-Pyr.).
³⁸ Béarnais.
³⁹ Old Prov.
⁴⁰ Old Prov.
⁴¹ E as in note 22.
⁴² Final a tends slightly toward an o; the initial vowel bears a vertical stroke under it.
⁴³ Béronie 991 remarks that this has also the extended meaning of 'all women of highest condition'.

daouno,⁴⁴ 1023 *daòunou* 1023, *done* 1030,⁴⁵ *damne* 1048, *dáwno* 1057, *dŏnĕ* 1068, *dōnă* 1068,⁴⁶ *daoune* 1100, *dona*,⁴⁷ *damée* 'woman just married',⁴⁸ *denĩ* 'mother-in-law',⁴⁹ *done* 'little girl',⁵⁰ *dŏn* 'young girl'.⁵¹ Mod. Fr. *donne* means 'woman' in a pejorative sense; Mid. Fr. and Mod. Fr. *dame* can mean 'nun'. ALF map 570 gives several forms in the dépt. of Gironde: *dūn* at 630,⁵² *dōn* at 632,⁵³ *dōne* at 641,⁵⁴ *dòne* at 662;⁵⁵ in Landes: *dòne* at 672.⁵⁶ ALF map 548 gives *dŏnà* at 992.⁵⁷ The general distribution is approximately as follows: *dam, damm, dame* in Normandie and Wallon regions; *danme* in Champagne; *daime* in Bourgogne; *dam, dem* on German border; *donne, dona, donno* on Swiss and Ital. borders; *dama, dana* in Dauphiné; *damna, dona, damo, dono* in Languedoc; *daune, dono, daouno, damo, dona, dono* in Gascogne.⁵⁸

⁴⁴ FEW Lief. 13.124, at Bayonne.

⁴⁵ In Bessin and Val de Saire (Manche) this means 'sorceress, ridiculous woman'; this form cited also by Hemmann op. cit.

⁴⁶ Griera's Catalan Ling. Atlas 1068 contains this spelling with a number of variants as to accent: short *e* with grave accent and long open *o*, long open *o* with close *e*, sometimes nasalized *o*, etc. In its source the term cited is printed with a short straight horizontal stroke crossing the upper part of the shaft of *d*, indicating that *d* tends toward *th;* however, *d* does not always tend toward *th* in the pronunciation of this term in this region. For second form from 1068 the *o* in some variants is open and bears either a grave or acute accent. *A* in some variants bears a grave accent; in one instance it tends toward *o*. *D* tends toward *th* and printed in source as in note 46.

⁴⁷ FEW Lief. 13.124, Ariège. *O* bears a small arc directly under it opening toward the right.

⁴⁸ FEW supra, Centre.

⁴⁹ FEW supra, Béarnais.

⁵⁰ FEW supra, Gironde. In source cited final *e* is printed as Fr. phonetic symbol for mute *e* and is placed between parentheses.

⁵¹ FEW supra, Landes.

⁵² *U* bears an acute accent.

⁵³ *O* bears an acute accent.

⁵⁴ *O* bears a grave accent. A form of the same spelling at 653 bears a grave accent over a short *o* and a dot over a small echo vowel *e*. In source cited this term bears a dot over the *e*.

⁵⁵ *O* is semi-nasal; *e* bears a dot over it.

⁵⁶ *O* is semi-nasal and bears a vertical stroke under it; *e* as in note 55.

⁵⁷ One of the two forms cited bears a vertical stroke under *o*.

⁵⁸ Consult also: Sainéan, ZRP 30.308; Baist, ZRP 32.45; Brüch, ZRP 41.584; Thomas, Romania 12.585.

Chapter VI

OTHER TERMS BUILT ON DOMINA AND TERMS BUILT ON DOMINICELLA

O. Fr. *damoisele* 'girl of the nobility; married woman of the petty nobility, even of the bourgeoisie' is derived from V. L. **domnicella (dŏmĭnĭcĕlla)*, a diminutive of *domina* meaning 'young girl'. In the 17th and 18th Cents. the word continued to express the idea of 'a girl of the nobility'; in contemporary French *demoiselle* is a 'woman who is not married',[1] or is used in addressing any young woman—a waitress, for instance. The O. Pr. *donsela* 'young girl' and the Mod. Pr. *damisello* 'demoiselle' are from the same source as the French forms.[2] Similarly *madamoiselle* was a title given to a girl or married woman of the petty nobility up to the 17th Cent., then, for a time, it was a 'title given to the daughter of the brother, or of the uncle, of the king'; in the 18th Cent. it became a 'title given to young girls'.[3] O. Fr. and Mid. Fr. *madame*, derived from *domina*, O. Pr. *madama*, Mod. Pr. *madamo*, was a 'title given to the wife of a noble', or to women of royal blood in the 17th Cent.; in Mod. Fr. it is a 'title given to every married woman'.[4] O. Pr. retains the forms *damixela, damaixela, domixela*, taken over from O. Fr. *demoiselle*, and equivalent to the latter in meaning.[5] O. Pr. *donsela* travelled north, leaving in O. Fr. the forms *donxele, danxele, dansele*, all meaning 'dame, demoiselle (with a nuance of scorn)'.[6] Good Mod. Eng. equivalents for the three major terms under discussion are: *demoiselle* 'young lady, unmarried lady, young girl, gentlewoman'; *madame* 'madam, mistress, Mrs.'; *mademoiselle* 'miss, Miss'.[7] In the following occurrences meanings have been cited only when there is a divergence from the general: *demoiselle* 29, *dammzel* 38, *dammuzelett* 38 'little demoiselle', *damehèle* 39 'maid servant of the farm who takes care of the cows', *dimwèxèle* 39, *damzelle* 57 'pretentious girl', *damzilette* 57 'coquettish young girl, gay working girl', *donzelle* 57 'girl of questionable morals', *damzel* 105 'demoiselle, girl of honest parents of the good bour-

---

[1] REW 2737; Gam. 289; FEW Lief. 13.133: cites Mid. Fr. *domnixelle* in the Eulalia; I. Pauli, 'Enfant', 'Garçon' et 'Fille' dans les langues romanes, 163.
[2] FEW Lief. 13.133.
[3] Id.
[4] REW 2733, Gam. 289 and 578, FEW Lief. 13.124.
[5] FEW Lief. 13.133.
[6] Id.
[7] P. Passy and G. Hempl, International Fr.-Eng. and Eng.-Fr. Dict., 171 and 366. Cotgrave cites *damoiselle* as 'a gentlewoman, anyone under the degree of Ladie, that wears, or may wear, a veluet hood'.

geois', *damzilett* 105 'gay working girl, young girl of the working class', *damhel* 82 'German-speaking maid-servant', *damhel* 84 'maid-servant',[8] *dimoizel* 105, *madame* 145, *mamzelet* 150 'little girl',[9] *dimoèzèle* 151 'name given to the institutrices of the communal schools' (an additional extended meaning), *mamzèle* 151, *madamoselle* 164, *damette* 226 'diminutive of dame', *damerette* 226 'pl. dim. of dame', *demoiselle* 226 'noblewoman', *demoisillons* 226 'pl. dim. of demoiselle', *doinzelles* 226 'demoiselles', *domzelles* 226 demoiselles', *mameselle* 233, *damillon* 233 'woman who affects the manners of a grande dame', *demoisalle* 264, *doncelle* 284, *damoiche* 360 'dim. of demoiselle', *demoiselle* 398 'title given to fairies, fantastic persons', *demoselle* 398, *demoiselle* 401, *dmwexel* 305 'demoiselle',[10] *demaxel* 320 'demoiselle',[11] *damwaxal* 320 'demoiselle', *demoselle* 388, *damoiselle* 424, *madamm* 38, *donzelle* 522, *donxelle* 522 'maid-servant, *demyal* 560 'servant, maid',[12] *demyol* 560,[13] *demyāl* 560,[14] *demyōl* 560,[15] *demwinzèle* (*d*[*e*]*mwezel*) 560,[16] *demwasèle* (*d*[*e*]*mwäzel*) 560 'institutrice',[17] *diemehale* (*dyemyal*) 560,[18] *mamsèle* (*mämzel*) 560 'miss, majaurée, précieuse',[19] *medmwēzel* 560,[20] *medmwezel* 560,[21] *demhale* 575 'maid-servant', *demyal* 581 'maid-servant',[22]

---

[8] *E* bears a close hook directly under it opening to the right, in source.
[9] Each *e* as in note 8.
[10] Each *e* as in note 8.
[11] In source initial *e* is printed as Fr. phonetic symbol for mute *e*.
[12] Messin patois at Vivy; Nied patois at Frécourt, Sorbey, and Remilly. Here *e* bears a hook under it opening to the left. As cited by Zéliqzon 560 this and the three forms following are phonetic; when actually written they are spelled identically *demehale*. All these forms have identical meanings.
[13] L'Isle patois at Maizières and Verny; Pays-Haut patois at Amanvillers and Gorze. *O* bears a close hook directly under it opening to the right.
[14] Sounois patois at Dieuze, Château-Salin, and Ommeray. *E* as in note 8.
[15] Vosgien patois at Gondrexange, Lorquin, and Réchicourt. *E* bears a hook under it opening to the left.
[16] Messin patois at Vigy; L'Isle patois at Maizières and Verny.
[17] Messin patois at Vigy; L'Isle patois at Maizières and Verny; Pays-Haut patois at Amanvillers and Gorze; Fentsch patois at Fontoy; Nied patois at Frécourt. The *e* in brackets bears a hook under it opening to the left. The following *a* bears a long mark directly over the diaeresis, in the source from which taken.
[18] Messin patois at Vigy. *E* in parenthetical term as in note 8.
[19] Messin patois at Vigy; L'Isle patois at Maizières and Verny; Pays-Haut patois at Amanvillers and Gorze; Nied patois at Frécourt, Sorbey, and Remilly. The *e* in the parenthetical word, in its source, is printed with an open hook directly under it opening to the right.
[20] Initial and final *e* as in note 8. Messin patois at Vigy; L'Isle patois at Maizières and Verny. This term and the one following are phonetic variations, both being actually written mèdemwinsèle according to Zéliqzon 560.
[21] Nied patois at Frécourt, Sorbey, and Remilly; Sounois patois at Dieuze, Château-Salin, and Ommeray; Vosgien patois at Gondrexange, Lorquin, and Réchicourt. Each *e* as in note 8.
[22] There is an echo vowel *o* between *a* and *l*; *e* as in note 8.

TERMS BUILT ON DOMINA AND DOMINICELLA 11

domhal 558 'maid-servant',[23] *daimmehalle* 598 'maid-servant', *domm'halle* 583 'maid-servant', *damhāl* 584 'maid-servant', *démoisêlle* 579, *medem* 620,[24] *dêmoisêlle* 580, *dŏzäl* 617 'maid-servant', *mzelle* 667, *mämzel* 560,[25] *dŏzala* 667 'maid-servant', *damusalla* 647, *donzela* 647 'young servant, little chambermaid',[26] *donzala* 647,[27] *donzelle* 667 'servant, chambermaid',[28] *demejala* 670 'demoiselle, girl of the nobility', *damuzala* 673 'demoiselle, *damuzo* 675 'young girl who busies herself with trifles', *damwésĕlă* 703,[29] *damwéslă* 703,[30] *dmwélà* 703,[31] *damwésëla* 713, *madamă* 703,[32] *demoiselle* 741 bis 'daughter', *madama* 759, *damoche* 745,[33] *domisella* 756, *madameisella* 764,[34] *donzella* 767, *damixela* 772,[35] *damüxela* 772, *damizella* 777, *madamuesella* 779, *madàma* 779, *damaiseleto* 788 'dim. of demoiselle', *damaisélo* 788,[36] *damisela* 788,[37] *damisèlo* 788,[38] *damisello* 788,[39] *damèiseloto* 788 'dim. of demoiselle',[40] *damiseleto* 788 'dim. of demoiselle',[41] *dameto* 789 'dim. of dame', *madouneto* 789 'woman of low condition', *madamo* 805, *damiseleto*

[23] *O* as in note 13.
[24] Each *e* as in note 8.
[25] *E* as in note 8.
[26] Bridel and Favrat 647 state that this word does not have a pejorative meaning in the bishopric of Bâle, but that in general *na donzala* signifies 'a woman or girl of equivocal virtue'.
[27] See note 19.
[28] Pierrehumbert 667 says that the term is current only in the patois at Neuch in the district of Boudry.
[29] At Albertville in the arr. of Albertville. The meaning is the same and the following terms from 703.
[30] At Epersy and Mognard in the arr. of Chambéry.
[31] At Leschaux in the arr. of Annecy.
[32] At Annecy in the arr. of Annecy.
[33] Puitspelu 745 defines this humorously: 'une dame qui n'est pas dame et qui veut faire la dame. Je ne connais rien de plus laid'.
[34] Champollion-Figeac 764 cites this from the vulgar language of Grenoble.
[35] This term and the one following from 772 each bears a dot directly under *e*.
[36] Azaïs 788 observes that this is a title common to all unmarried daughters of a family and that formerly it was applied only to girls of noble birth.
[37] Id.
[38] Id.
[39] Id.
[40] E. L. Adams, Word-Formation in Provençal, 391: '*-el* is another suffix which was very frequently combined with other suffixes, particularly *-et;* the ending *-elet* being of common occurrence in Provençal', and 'the words ending in *-el* were thought of as simple words, and a new suffix *-et* was added'. F. Mistral, Dictionnaire Provençal-Français 1.695 cites a number of other related derivations: Gasc. *dausèro, doumaisello;* Dauph. *demeisello;* Vivarais *dumisello;* Marseillais *damiseloto, dameiseloto;* Limousin *doumaiseloto;* and the following used as adjectives and substantives: *dameiselen, doumeiselenc, doumaiselenc, doumaiselenco,* having the meaning of 'that which belongs or has reference to *demoiselles* or that which affects their adjustment'.
[41] See note 40.

838, *doumaiseleto* 866 'young demoiselle', *madamo* 805, *damiseleto* 838, *doumaiseleto* 866 'young demoiselle', *madamo* 871 'young woman of the middle class', *doumaisélo* 916, *doumaixèlo* 920, *madoumaïselo* 921, *domasso* 940 'large woman', *dounzèlo* 940 'girl of evil life', *madamo* 921 'married woman', *madàmo* 962, *demeisello* 968, *damisela* 975,[42] *damouisellao* 975,[43] *duègno* 940 'old, ugly woman',[44] *douógno* 940 'old, ugly woman',[45] *madamwizéla* 978,[46] *dameto* 980 'woman of inferior rank, dim. of dame', *dameisèlo* 987, *doumeiselo* 991 'daughter of an honest family',[47] *madâmo* 987, *madame* 989, *meixelou* 991 'young demoiselle', *damésèllo* 949, *demwixella* 978,[48] *madàma* 978,[49] *made* 871 'madame', *dora* 956 'maid of honor at a wedding', *doumeyjèlo* 1008, *modamo* 1008, *dausere* 1020 'demoiselle', *madona* 1020, *damasysèleto* 1023, *damasysèlo* 1023, *damayselotto* 1023 'young demoiselle', *doumisel* 1023,[50] *mamiselle* 1030, *damiselle* 1030, *damaïselo* 1044, *doumayzèlo* 1044,[51] *madame* 1047, *damisèle* 1094, *damoiselles*,[52] *damioche* 'bourgeois woman who wants to imitate a great lady',[53] *daunino* 'dim. of dame',[54] *damillon* 'woman who affects the manners of a great lady',[55] *midan* 'madam, title given to the wife of a noble',[56] *midon* 'madame, title given to the wife of a noble',[57] *madona*,[58] *maidaime*,[59] *medem*,[60] *madama*,[61] *madamo*,[62] *midono*

---

[42] Piémontais.

[43] Auvergnat.

[44] Mod. Fr. *duegne*, all these from Sp. *dueña* 'old woman who watches over a young girl', see FEW Lief. 13.126.

[45] Id.

[46] All of the *a*'s tend slightly toward *o*; *e* bears a vertical stroke directly under it.

[47] Béronie 991 remarks: 'Autrefois dans les villes, et encore aujourd'hui dans les campagnes, on appellait aussi doumeisello les femmes mariées d'une contraire condition'.

[48] In its source initial *e* is printed as the Fr. phonetic symbol for mute *e*; second *e* bears a dot directly under it; final *a* tends toward *o*.

[49] The first and last *a*'s tend slightly toward *o*; second *a* bears a vertical stroke directly under it.

[50] Durrieux 1023 wrongly supposes this to be from the Gr. σαμαλίς, σαμαλίζα, and comments: 'Littré, Brachet et Scheler inventent un hideux barbarisme *dominicellus* pour le dériver du latin'. *Dominicellus*, however, has been attested, see REW 2737.

[51] See note 40 for this term, for the one immediately following and for all those from 1023.

[52] See J. Brütting, Das Bauern-Französisch in Dancourts Lustspielen.

[53] Poitevin, see FEW Lief. 13.124.

[54] Béarnais, FEW loc. cit.

[55] Le Havre, FEW loc. cit.

[56] Bresse (12th-16th Cents.), FEW loc. cit.

[57] Old Dauph., FEW loc. cit.

[58] Old Béarnais, FEW loc. cit.

[59] Loches (Indre-et-Loire), FEW loc. cit.

[60] Montbéliard (Doubs), FEW loc. cit. Each *e* bears a tiny open hook directly under it opening to the right.

[61] Annecy (H.-Savoie), FEW loc. cit.

[62] Languedocien, FEW loc. cit.

'foreign lady or woman',[63] *mâme* 'madame',[64] *mame*,[65] *mas* 'madame',[66] *midomna* 'engaged girl, newly-married woman',[67] *damexél*,[68] *moiselle* 'demoiselle',[69] *demoselle*,[70] *dmwĕxel*,[71] *dmwĕxel*,[72] *dmwéla*,[73] *domisella*,[74] *damixela*,[75] *doumèisélo*,[76] *dõxel*,[77] *moisillon* 'term of scorn for a girl of mediocre condition who has a distaste for the work of keeping house',[78] *(de)moisillon* 'peasant girl who apes the toilette of the demoiselle of the city',[79] *doumeiselenc* 'one who affects demoiselle airs',[80] *madamwéla*,[81] *madamisello*,[82] *mamoiselle*,[83] *mameselle*,[84] *mamzelle*,[85] *mamzel*,[86] *mam'zulète* 'dim. of demoiselle',[87] *demoiselle* 'daughter',[88] *demoiselle* 'suivante',[89] *demiselle* 'maidservant',[90] *damhel*,[91] *donxala*,[92] *demxal*,[93] *demxol*,[94] *demxāl*,[95] *dèm'hole*,[96]

[63] Limousin, FEW loc. cit.
[64] Paris, FEW loc. cit.
[65] Picardie and Artois, FEW loc. cit.
[66] Limousin, FEW loc. cit.
[67] Bretagne, FEW loc. cit.
[68] Vannes, FEW loc. cit.
[69] Picardie, FEW loc. cit.
[70] Loches (Indre-et-Loire), FEW loc. cit.
[71] Metz (Moselle), FEW loc. cit. Second *e* bears an open hook directly under it opening to the right.
[72] Isle (Moselle), FEW loc. cit. Second *e* as in note 71.
[73] Thônes, FEW loc. cit.
[74] St. Estienne (Loire), FEW loc. cit.
[75] Villette-Serpaize (Isère, Vienne), FEW loc. cit. *E* as in note 8.
[76] Languedocien, FEW loc. cit.
[77] Jura Bernois (Switz.); *donxelle* at Paris means 'girl of equivocal virtue', FEW loc. cit. *E* as in note 35.
[78] Picardie, FEW loc. cit.
[79] Norman, FEW loc. cit.
[80] Languedocien, FEW loc. cit.
[81] Annecy (H.-Savoie), FEW loc. cit.
[82] Mod. Prov., FEW loc. cit.
[83] Paris, FEW loc. cit.
[84] Mod. Fr., FEW loc. cit.
[85] Paris, rare, FEW loc. cit.
[86] Breton, FEW loc. cit.
[87] Louvain (Belgium), FEW loc. cit.
[88] Paris and Norman, FEW loc. cit.
[89] Mod. Fr. and Mons (Belgium), FEW loc. cit.
[90] Old Lorraine; the following twelve terms have this meaning, FEW loc. cit.
[91] Louvain and Metz (Moselle), FEW loc. cit.
[92] Old Lorraine, FEW loc. cit.
[93] Nied (Moselle), FEW loc. cit. In its source *x* is printed as a capital *x* in italics and *e* as the Fr. phonetic symbol for mute *e*.
[94] Pays-Haut and Isle (Moselle), FEW loc. cit. *E* as in note 8, *o* as in note 13.
[95] Sounois, FEW loc. cit. *E* as in note 8, *x* as in note 93.
[96] Le Tholy (Vosges), FEW loc. cit.

demhale,[97] *demhal*,[98] *demmjalle*,[99] *demzal*,[100] *deum'hale*,[101] *demzol*,[102] *dõzala*,[103] *dounzèle* 'maid of honor at a wedding',[104] *dounzelle*,[105] *demoiselle* 'woman in the service of an establishment, of an administration',[106] *dmwäzel* 'institutrice',[107] *damoisele* 'proprietress of a house of prostitution, prostitute, concubine of a priest',[108] *moiselle*,[109] *demoiselle*,[110] *damisello*,[111] *dounzèlo*,[112] *damisella*,[113] *demoiselle* 'title for fairies, fantastic persons',[114] *mamesèle* 'mijaurée, précieuse, city woman',[115] *daumoise* 'hussy',[116] *doncella*,[117] *donzella* 'virgin'.[118]

[97] Fraize (Vosges), FEW loc. cit.
[98] Neuwiler (Bas-Rhin), FEW loc. cit.
[99] La Poutroie (Haut-Rhin), FEW loc. cit.
[100] La Baroche (Haut-Rhin), FEW loc. cit. *E* as in note 8; *z* bears a small v-shaped symbol directly above it.
[101] La Bresse (Vosges), FEW loc. cit.
[102] *E* as in note 93; *z* as in note 100. South Vosges, FEW loc. cit.
[103] Jura Bernois; Wartburg explains that this meaning 'maid-servant' is limited to the east, to the border dialects, being in existence in 1300, in Switz. since the 13th Cent., having no direct connection with the change of meaning which this word has passed through in the written lang.; FEW loc. cit.
[104] Béarnais, obs., FEW loc. cit.
[105] Landes, obs., FEW loc. cit. Meaning same as that of preceding term.
[106] Mod. Fr., obs., FEW loc. cit.
[107] *E* as in note 8. Moselle, obs., FEW loc. cit.
[108] O. Fr. and Mod. Fr. (14th-16th Cents.), obs., FEW loc. cit.
[109] Picardie; the following four terms have this meaning.
[110] Blois, FEW loc. cit.
[111] Mod. Pr., FEW loc. cit.
[112] Aveyron, FEW loc. cit.
[113] Catalan, see Pauli 166; this also has regular meaning, FEW loc. cit.
[114] Centre, FEW loc. cit.
[115] Moselle, FEW loc. cit.
[116] Anjou, FEW loc. cit.
[117] Catalan, see REW 2737, FEW loc. cit.
[118] Catalan, see Pauli 166, FEW loc. cit.

Chapter VII

FEMELLA

Fr. *femelle* is derived from Latin *femella* 'female', and from the dim. of *femme* 'little woman, wife'.[1] The Lat. form is considered a dim. of *femina*: **femen-(e)la*. The suffix normally *-ella* remained *-el(l)e* in French. Dialect and patois occurrences of *femelle* are: *frumel* 38 'female as opposed to male', *femelette* 57 'woman with neither health nor experience',[2] *fumlett* 105 'femmelette, femme très simple, d'un esprit bonne et d'humeur légère' *femelle* 198, 398 'woman, girl', 411, 622, *fĕmlēt* 204 'woman who doesn't know how to work or manage her household',[3] *fémelle* 208, *fŭmēl* 286,[4] *fumelle* 356, 384 'woman, woman who leads an evil life', 394, 397 'woman (in a jolly, broad, or off-color sense)', 419 'woman, female, maîtresse',[5] 445 'female, woman, girl', *fūmelle* 522, *fămāl* 541,[6] *f(e)mel* 560,[7] *femel* 560,[8] *femal* 560,[9] *femel* 560,[10] *femēl* 560,[11] *fèmèl* 590,[12] *femèle* 628, *f'mélo* 628, *fumèle* 628,[13] *fumélo* 628,[14] *femelet* 640, *femalla* 647, 758 'woman, wife',

---

[1] REW 3238; Kt. 3678; also see A. Ernout and A. Meillet, Dictionnaire étymologique de la langue latine, 329: **femella, -ae*, very rare, three examples in Catullus, but preserved in Fr. and Prov., means 'little woman'.

[2] This and all similar occurrences in *-ette, -et, -ote, -eto*, represent the addition of regular Latin dim. suffixes, and in these particular cases we have what is equivalent to a double diminutive. Cf. Grandgent, Latín vulgar (Moll.) 41–50.

[3] The first *e* bears an acute accent directly above the long mark and the second *e* bears a grave accent directly above the short mark in the source consulted.

[4] *E* as second *e* in note 3.

[5] Canton of Variennes-sur-Allier (Allier).

[6] *oe* and *e* bear grave accents in source consulted.

[7] Messin patois at Vigy; Nied patois at Frécourt, Sorbey, and Remilly. *E* in parentheses bears a hook under it opening to the left; second *e* bears a short close hook directly under it opening toward right and top, in source consulted.

[8] L'Isle patois at Maizières and Verny; Pays-Haut patois at Amanvillers and Gorze. Both *e*'s as second *e* in note 7.

[9] Fentsch patois at Fontoy. *E* bears an open rounded hook directly under it and opening to the right, in source consulted.

[10] Saunois patois at Dieuze, Château-Salin, and Ommeray; first *e* bears a hook under it opening to the left; second *e* as in note 9.

[11] Occurrences as in note 10, also in patois vosgien at Gondrexange, Lorquin, and Réchicourt. First *e* as in note 10.

[12] Also in *-el* in district 12 and *-äl* in district 26.

[13] Vitteaux (Côte-d'Or).

[14] Mesnay (Jura).

16 WORDS AND DESCRIPTIVE TERMS FOR 'WOMAN' AND 'GIRL'

femala 670, 672, 675 'woman (in a general sense)', *femeleta* 675 'frail and delicate', *fmla* 701, *fĕmală* 703,[15] *fmală* 703,[16] *femëla* 703,[17] *fèmèlà* 711, *fetmella* 715, *fumâla* 721, *femeleto* 789 'charming little woman', *femelote* 789 'little woman', *femèlo* 890, 962, *fuméla* 978,[18] *fumelo* 1022, 1044, *fimèlo* 1044.

The following items from the FEW have the regular meaning of Fr. *femelle* 'être de sexe féminin': *fumelle*,[19] *femela*,[20] *femelle*,[21] *frumelle*,[22] *fümel*,[23] *feumelle*,[24] *fumèle*,[25] *femalle*,[26] *fmel*,[27] *femel*,[28] *femala*,[29] *femella*,[30] *fmala*,[31] *fümela*,[32] *fümélo*,[33] *femèlo*,[34] *fumèlo*,[35] *feimélo*,[36] *femèle*,[37] *fimêle*.[38]

The FEW also contains a number of these terms under the heading 'femme, personne de sexe fémenin' (familiarly and in derision already in the 17th Cent.): *femelle*,[39] *fumelle*,[40] *fumméle*,[41] *fuméle* 'woman of evil life',[42]

[15] Balme-de-Sellingy in arr. of Annecy.
[16] Thônes in arr. of Annecy.
[17] Mondane in arr. of Saint-Jean-de-Maurienne.
[18] *E* bears a vertical stroke directly under it; final *a* tends slightly toward *o*.
[19] This term occurs in O. Fr., Mid. Fr., at Mons (Belgium), in Picard, at Provins (Seine-et-Marne), and at Varennes-sur-Allier (Allier). For this term and those following see FEW Lief. 21.447-9.
[20] O. Prov.
[21] Paris, also fumelle.
[22] Louvain.
[23] Namur (Belgium) and in Norman; in latter occurrence *e* is as in note 9.
[24] Varennes-sur-Allier (Allier).
[25] Lacrost (Saône-et-Loire), Minot (Côte-d'Or).
[26] Domecy-sur-le-Vault (Yonne).
[27] Metz (Moselle). *E* as in note 9.
[28] At Isle (Moselle) and at Pays-Haut (Moselle) first *e* is as in note 9, second *e* as second *e* in note 7. At Saunois (Moselle) first *e* of this term is printed in source consulted as Fr. phonetic symbol for mute *e*, second *e* as just explained above.
[29] Swiss. In source *e* is printed as Fr. phonetic symbol for mute *e*.
[30] Montana (Valais, Switz.). First *e* as in note 29; second *e* as second *e* in note 7.
[31] Savoie, H.-Savoie.
[32] Terres-Froides (region around Virieu and Isère). *E* as in note 9.
[33] Trièves (Isère). *E* bears a long mark under it and a hook opening to the right.
[34] Toulouse (H.-Garonne).
[35] Lavelanet (Ariège), Chavanat (Creuse).
[36] Mauriac (Cantal).
[37] Béarn., also *fumèle*.
[38] La Teste-de-Buch (Gironde).
[39] At Paris and Pays de Bray (Seine-Inf.).
[40] At Paris this has its regular meaning and that of 'prostitute'; in Norman it has the usual meaning with pejorative connotation; at Pont-Audemer (Eure); at Bellême (Orne); at Alençon (Orne); at Dol (Ille-et-V.); at Jublains (Mayenne) it means 'young girl'; in Anjou it has a pejorative connotation; at Chef-Boutonne (Deux-Sèvres) it means 'girl'; in Saintonge and in Aunis it means 'girl'; in the regions bordering the Seudre and the Seugne rivers it means 'girl'; at La Rochelle (Charente-Inf.) it means 'girl' (here the term *femelle* also occurs); in the Centre

FEMELLA 17

fumèle,[43] *fœmel*,[44] *feumelle*,[45] *femále*,[46] *femala*,[47] *femā*,[48] *femalla*,[49] *femelá*,[50] *females*,[51] *fmēlã*,[52] *fémala*,[53] *femēla*,[54] *fumela*,[55] *fümela*,[56] *fümèla*,[57] *füméla*,[58] *fümele*,[59] *fmela*,[60] *femelo*,[61] *fumèla*,[62] *femaletta* 'petite femme',[63] *femelan* 'les femmes en général',[64] *fumelan*,[65] *femelun*,[66] *fumelis*.[67]

---

region it means 'girl' as well as its usual meaning; in Berry it means 'woman' with the special nuance of 'woman of evil life'; at Loches (Indre-et-Loire) it means 'woman' with the special nuance of 'woman of evil life'; at Sancoins (Cher); at Varennes-sur-Allier (Allier); at Clairvaux (Aube) it means 'woman' with scornful connotation; in the Argonne it means 'woman' with scornful connotation.

[41] Démuin (Somme).
[42] Bessin (Calvados).
[43] La Hague (Manche), usually with pejorative connotation.
[44] Bas-Maine. *Œ* bears a dot under it. *Fümel* also occurs with the same meaning and, in addition, that of 'maîtresse'.
[45] In Haute-Maine this term has the meaning of 'young girl'. Here also *fumelle* occurs. At Coutouvre (Loire).
[46] Freibourg (Switz.). First *e* as in note 9; second *e* same except hook extends only half as far below the letter.
[47] Waadt (Swiss canton); *e* as in note 29. Blonay (Waadt, Switz); in this occurrence *e* bears a dot under it.
[48] Val de Bagnes (Valais, Switz.). *E* as in note 29.
[49] Aosta (Italy).
[50] Val Saona (Italy). Each *e* as in note 29.
[51] Savoie, Haute-Savoie. The term is plural.
[52] Aussois (Savoie). *E* bears a grave accent over the long mark and a hook under it opening to the right.
[53] Albertville (Savoie). This term also means 'girl'.
[54] Bessans (Savoie) with pejorative meaning. Second *e* bears an acute accent over it and a dot under it; final *a* tends slightly towards *o*.
[55] Lyon, used pejoratively.
[56] Dauphiné, Balme (French-speaking region in Piémont, Italy) with scornful connotation.
[57] Crémieu (Isère); this term also has the meaning 'concubine'. *E* bears a dot under it.
[58] Ala di Stura (Piémont, prov. Torino, Italy). *E* bears a hook under it opening to the right.
[59] Pragelato (Piémont, Italy). This and the following three terms signify 'woman' with pejorative connotation. First *e* as in note *9;* final *e* as in note 29.
[60] Usseglio (Franco-Provençal-speaking region in Piémont, Italy). *E* as in note 9.
[61] Mod. Prov. and Languedoc.
[62] Champsaur (district in H.-Alpes), Lallé (in St. Jacques community in H.-Alpes).
[63] Aosta (Italy).
[64] Mod. Prov., Barcelonnette (B.-Alpes), the word here is masc.; see also Piém *fumlam;* also at Marseille and in B.-Dauphiné; the term cited and the following terms have the meaning 'woman in general'.
[65] Champsaur (H.-Alpes), Mod. Prov. and Languedoc.
[66] Dauphiné, Pézenas (Hérault), Aveyron, also *fumelun*.
[67] Béarn., here masc. sg.

See ALF Map 547 'femelle', which contains largely these same forms with varying stresses and accents.[68]

[68] See also ALF 548 (some scattered forms), 376 'belle dame' at 513 and 967, and also map 570 'fille' at 411.

CHAPTER VIII

FEMME

Femme is accepted as being derived from Latin *femina*,¹ which originally in C. L. meant 'female', but which preserved only the meaning of 'woman' in Gallo-Romance. It took on the added meaning of 'wife' in standard French.² The O. Fr. form *feme*, of the same derivation, was used in the particularized sense of 'femme de mauvaise vie' in such phrasesas *feme de vie* and *feme du monde*.³ The O. Pr. form *femna* had the same meaning as the Mod. Fr.; this is also true of the Mod. Pr. form of the same spelling.⁴

Occurrences in the dialects and patois are as follows: *fremo* 2, 786,⁵ 828, 805, 848,⁶ *fame* 25, 226, *feumm* 38, *fem* 81,⁷ *fem* 82, 131, *feum* 105, *feume* 111, 146, *fem* 136, 452, *fèm'* 139, *fœm* 150, 290,⁸ *feùme* 151, *faimme* 176, *feme* 198, 375, *femme*,⁹ 198, 208, 269, 302, 334, 398, 411, 745,¹⁰ *fenme* 198, *fàm* 204,¹¹ *fẽm* 204,¹² *fem* 204,¹³ *fóm* 286,¹⁴ *fom* 290, *fum* 307, 320, *fene* 419, 811, 816, *fenne* 423, 424, 745,¹⁵ 805,¹⁶ *fena*,¹⁷ 425, 670, 672, 675, 678, 679, 682, 742, 755, 756, 767, 775, 779, 780, 788,¹⁸ 810, 901, *fanne* 426, 607, *fonne* 433, 448, 454, 620, 628,¹⁹ *fam*,²⁰ 435, 495, 518, 542, 560,²¹ 616, *fan-ne*

---

[1] REW 3239; Diez 582; Bloch 1.294; Littré, op. cit. 2.1639 gives an untenable derivation: *fœmina* (Gr. μένη); Kt. 3679; FEW Lief. 21.449.

[2] Bloch 1.201.

[3] Godefroy, Dict. de l'anc. lang. fr. 3.746.

[4] See note 2.

[5] In use from Nice to Bayonne.

[6] Aix.

[7] *E* bears a hook under it opening to right and top.

[8] Wallon.

[9] Paris; means also 'femme de mœurs légères'.

[10] Means 'femme du Puy'.

[11] *A* bears a long mark directly over it and just below the grave accent.

[12] This is the pronunciation of a large number of individuals; *e* bears a grave accent.

[13] The pronunciation in the faubourgs and banlieus.

[14] *O* bears a short mark directly over it and just beneath the accent.

[15] Obs.

[16] Patois of Pragelas valley in Dauphiné.

[17] Old Wald., Freibourg, Lyon, Dauphiné.

[18] 16th and 17th Cent. forms.

[19] Vitteaux (Côte d'Or).

[20] Vosges.

[21] Fentsch patois at Fontoy.

443, 614, *foune*,[22] 445, *fanme* 453, 501, *fan* 459, *fomme*,[23] 467, 478,[24] 532,[25] 580, 597, 579, 583, *fonme* 478,[26] *foume* 532,[27] 548, foumme 532,[28] faume 532,[29] fôme,[30] 532,[31] *fome*, 532,[32] 579, *fom* 590,[33] *feum'* 553, *fom*,[34] 560,[35] 594,[36] *fom* 560,[37] *fom* 590,[38] *fom* 594,[39] *fo:m* 594,[40] *fenna*,[41] 601, 647, 726, 731, 756, 758, 759, 764, 777, 780, 805,[42] 878, 975,[43] 988, *fènna* 601, *fanno* 601, *fannè* 601, *hembra* 601, *fãn*,[44] 604, 622, *fon·ne* 614, *fane* 623, *fono* 628,[45] *fana* 640, 751, *féne* 674,[46] *fené* 682, *fëna* 703,[47] *fèna* 703,[48] *fen* 703,[49] *fẽne* 709,[50] *fenà* 711,[51] *feinna* 715, *fëna* 721, *fena*,[52] 725, *femmena* 729, *fuma*

[22] Uchon (Saône et-Loire).
[23] Redon (Ille-et-Vilaine).
[24] Alliancelles; means 'fille'.
[25] At Ventron, Le Tholy, Mailly, and Landremont.
[26] Béru.
[27] Malzéville and Domgermain.
[28] See note 27.
[29] Longuet, Rehérey, and Vittel.
[30] 'Grande complainte, faite en vieux patois de la Bresse sur la vie de Frère Joseph Le Saint ermite de Ventron', in Rev. de phil. fr. et de lit. 1.248–57.
[31] Same as note 29.
[32] Old Bourgogne; Ventron, Le Tholy, Mailly, and Landremont.
[33] *O* bears a short mark directly over it.
[34] Pays-Haut; *o* bears a small hook directly under it opening to top and right.
[35] Messin patois at Vigy; l'Isle patois at Maizières and Verny; Sounois patois at Dieuze, Château-Salin, and Ommeray; Nied patois.
[36] Saint-Bresson.
[37] Vosges patois at Gondrexange, Lorquin, and Réchicourt; Sounois patois at Dieuze, Château-Salin, and Ommeray; *o* bears a long mark directly over it.
[38] There are two *o* forms from 590; each *o* bears a long mark directly over it, while one bears an acute accent and the other a grave accent directly over the long mark.
[39] Saint-Bresson; *o* printed in source as *e* symbol opening to left.
[40] Val d'Ajol; *o* as in note 39.
[41] Old Dauph.; Possoz, 'Chanson en patois de Séez (Savoie)', in Rev. de phil. fr. et de lit. 1.226–8.
[42] Old Vaudois, in Dauphiné.
[43] Auvergnat.
[44] Franche-Comté.
[45] Mesnay in Jura.
[46] Initial *e* bears a short mark directly over it and under the accent mark; final *e* in source is printed as Fr. phonetic symbol for mute *e*.
[47] Thônes in arr. of Annecy, in Savoy; Albertville in arr. of Albertville, in Savoy; Marthod in arr. of Albertville, in Savoy; *a* bears a short mark directly over it.
[48] Samoëns in arr. of Bonneville, in Savoy; *a* as in note 47.
[49] Genève, dialect of Certoux.
[50] *E* as in note 46.
[51] *E* bears a short mark directly over it.
[52] Sav., Suisse Romande, Aosta (Piémont, Italy).

FEMME 21

733, *fena* 749,[53] *fena* 751,[54] *fen'* 760,[55] *fene* 760,[56] *fema*,[57] 767,[58] *fena* 773,[59] *femno* 786,[60] 788,[61] *fenno*,[62] 786,[63] 865, 871, 890, 891, 892, 903, 915, 921, 940, 960, 962, 970, 990, 997, 1008, 1044, *femo* 786,[64] 838, 1044, *fumo* 786,[65] *frumo* 786,[66] *femeno* 788,[67] 789, 991, *hemne* 788,[68] 1034, 1035, 1088, 1090, 1093, 1094, 1100, 1101, *femna*,[69] 788,[70] 975,[71] 1009, *fembra* 788,[72] *feno* 805,[73] *feyno* 805,[74] 813, *frema*,[75] 858, *fénno* 880, 1015, *henno* 892, 1022, 1044, 1057, *fennos* 900, 1065, *fenno* 902,[76] *fenne* 902,[77] *fenno* 902,[78] *féãna* 956,[79] *feãna* 956, *fénno* 967,[80] *finna* 972, *fomna* 975,[81] *fēna* 978,[82] *feinno* 987, *fenne* 989, *fenno* 991,[83] *fénna* 1015,[84] *fèn'na* 1015, *fémo* 1015, *hemno* 1022, 1047, *heumne*

[53] *E* bears a dot directly under it.
[54] *E* bears a wavy line directly under it.
[55] *E* as in note 54.
[56] *E* as in note 54.
[57] Old Dauph., Old Freibourg., Dombres (Ain).
[58] 15th Cent. form.
[59] *E* as in note 46.
[60] In use from Nice to Bayonne.
[61] Haut- and Bas-Languedoc.
[62] Toulouse.
[63] In use from Nice to Bayonne.
[64] See note 63.
[65] See note 63.
[66] See note 63.
[67] Bas-Limousin.
[68] Béarn.
[69] F. Hemmann, Consonantismus des Gascognischen bis zum ende des dreizehnten Jahrhunderts.
[70] Old Catalan, masc. gender, means 'woman in general'.
[71] Auvergnat.
[72] See note 70.
[73] Old Briançonnais.
[74] Patois of Alpes Cottiennes: Briançonnais, Vallées Vaudoises, Queyras in particular.
[75] Nice.
[76] Eastern part of Languedoc-Catalonia frontier. Rousillon (general), southeastern and southwestern Narbonnais. *E* bears a small hook directly under it opening to right and top; *o* bears a dot directly under it and a small circle under the dot.
[77] Eastern part of the Languedoc-Catalonia frontier; Fenouillet, initial *e* as in note 76, final *e* as in note 46.
[78] Eastern part of Languedoc-Catalonia frontier; Montfort and northern section in general. *E* and *o* each bears a dot directly under it, and *o* bears a small circle below the dot.
[79] *E* as in note 46.
[80] *E* bears a vertical stroke directly under it.
[81] Piémontais.
[82] *E* bears a vertical stroke directly under it; *a* tends slightly toward *o*.
[83] *E* bears a long mark directly above it.
[84] *A* bears a long mark directly above it.

1032, *hemme* 1034, *haemne* 1036, *henne* 1078, *énna* 1068,[85] *femne*,[86] 1094, *hemble* 1094, *heno* 1098, *hemna* 1098, *finno*,[87] *fempna*,[88] *fempne*,[89] *femma*,[90] *fẽm*,[91] *fome*,[92] *femie*,[93] *fom*,[94] *fend*,[95] *fremo*,[96] *fréma*,[97] *fœnno*,[98] *fúmna*,[99] *fna*,[100] *feno*,[101] *fenna*,[102] *fam*,[103] *henno*,[104] *hemne*,[105] *hémna*.[106]

ALF map 548 'femme' shows the following general distribution: *fàm, fàm, fan, fóm, fóm* in northeastern France;[107] *fẽm, fèm, fàm, fèm* in northern France and along the Belgian border;[108] *fóm, fóm, fam, fàm* in eastern France and along the German border;[109] *fènà, fenà, fèn, fènà* along the Swiss border,[110] *fènà, fǽnà, féno, frèmè, frèmó, fǽmò* in southeastern France;[111]

[85] *E* bears a long mark over it and a vertical stroke directly under it; *a* bears a short mark directly over it.
[86] Hemmann, op. cit.
[87] M. Blanchet, Proverbes limousins, in Rev. de phil. fr. et de lit. 1.221–5.
[88] Hemann, op. cit.
[89] Ibid.
[90] E. P. L. Philipon, Dialectes bressans, in Rev. de phil. fr. et de lit. 1.30–55.
[91] Picardie.
[92] Old Bourgogne.
[93] Old Béarnais.
[92] Fougerolles (Haute-Saône); *o* bears a small hook directly under it opening to right and top.
[95] Val Soana (Canavese)—Franco-Prov. dialect of Piémont; see note 46 for initial *e*.
[96] Pietraporzio and Pontechianale, both in Piémont province; Cuneo, Italy. In the latter locality the meaning is 'dame'; *e* as in note 78.
[97] Barcelonnette (Basses-Alpes).
[98] Pral (Wald. dialect of Piémont).
[99] Noasca (Piémont, prov. Torino, Italy).
[100] See note 87.
[101] Trièves (Isère); *e* as in note 78.
[102] Wald. (Piémont); *e* as note 76.
[103] Vosges dépt.; *a* tends to *o*.
[104] Gascon; *e* as in note 78.
[105] Fougerolles (Haute-Saône); initial *e* as in note 78, final *e* as in note 46.
[106] Val d'Aran.
[107] Each vowel in the first and fourth forms bears a long mark directly over it just beneath the written accent; each vowel in the second and fifth forms bears a short mark directly over it.
[108] Each vowel in the second and third forms bears a long mark directly over it and just beneath the written accent mark; the fourth form bears a wavy line or tilde over the vowel.
[109] The vowel of the first form bears a wavy line or tilde directly over it; the vowel in the second form and in the fourth form bears a long mark directly over it; the vowel in the third form bears a short mark directly over it.
[110] *E* of first form bears a long mark directly over it and just under written accent; it also bears a vertical stroke directly under the letter. *E* of second form bears a short mark directly over it. *E* of third form bears a long mark directly over it just under the written accent mark; this third form has a tiny echo vowel *a* printed in

hǽmne, hemne, hemne, hǽmne, henno along the Spanish border;[112] *fena, fenà, fǽnó* along the Italian border;[113] *fàm, fàm, fèm* in northwestern France;[114] *fàn, fàm, fàn* in central France.[115]

Of the words cited throughout this chapter the general meaning is 'woman', 'wife', 'female' except where otherwise indicated.

The regular development of *femina* into French is **fem'na > femme*, the *-mn-* assimilating to *-mm-*. In the northeastern part of France, in the departments of Meuse, Meurthe-et-Moselle, Vosges, and along the German border the development was to *-om, -oum*, generally one syllable with no final vowel, though there are some cases in these regions of a development to *-anne*, a form common in other sections of the country. In south central France the most common development was to *-emna, -enna, -enno*; in the departments of Puy-de-Dôme and Haute-Loire there occurs a rather infrequent nasalization of the *-a-* and of the *-e-* in some cases, resulting in *-ẽna, -ãna*, etc. In southeastern France, in the departments of Vaucluse, Bas-du-Rhône, and in the west, forms in *-emeno* and *-énno* occur as well as forms with the intrusive *r* giving *fremo* and *frumo*.[116] The ending in *o*

---

the source as the final letter. *E* of fourth form bears a short mark directly over it just under the written accent mark; in the source this fourth form also has a small *n* printed after *n* here shown.

[111] *E* of first form bears a short mark over it just under written accent mark; it also bears a vertical stroke directly under the letter. *Œ* of second form bears a short mark over it just under written accent mark; it also bears a vertical stroke directly under the letter. *E* of third form bears a short mark over it just under written accent mark; it also bears a vertical stroke directly under the letter. Initial *e* of fourth form bears a short mark over it just under written accent mark. Each vowel of fifth form bears a short mark over it just under written accent mark. *Œ* of sixth form bears a short mark directly over it; there is also a vertical stroke under each of the vowels.

[112] *Œ* of first form bears a short mark directly over it just under written accent mark; in source final *e* of first form is printed as tiny echo vowel with dot directly above it.

[113] *E* of first form bears a short mark over it and a vertical stroke under it; *n* of first form is preceded by a tiny echo *n*. *E* of second form bears a short mark over it just under written accent mark; there is a tiny *n* placed as in first form. *Œ* of third form bears a short mark above it just under written accent mark.

[114] *A* of first form bears a long mark over it just under written accent mark; *a* of second form bears a short mark over it just under written accent mark; *e* of third form bears a wavy line or tilde over it just under written accent mark.

[115] *A* of first form bears a short mark over it just under written accent mark; *a* of second form bears a long mark over it just under written accent mark; *a* of third form bears a mark over it indicating semi-nasalization.

[116] The intrusive *r* is an occasional development in the Provençal regions of France and Italy, witness such examples as: *fulgure* (short mark over each *u*) > (Neap.) *fruvole* (dot under *o*) (REW 3555); *funda* (short mark over *u*) > (Pied.) *franda*, (Mod. Fr.) *fronde*, (Prov. and Cat.) *fronda* (REW 3577); *fustis* (long mark over *u*) > Prov. *frustar* (REW 3618).

is common in these regions as well as farther west and south in the departments of Hérault, Aude, and Gard. In the departments of Landes and Basses-Pyrénées developments to *-emne* and *-eumne* are frequent, with the initial *h*, a phenomenon occurring also in Spain. Generally in the northwestern part of the country we find the standard development *femme*, beside forms in *-om* and *-um*. In the west central and north central departments *femme* is usual. Along the Belgian border *-eum*, *-em*, *-èm* are common, and in the regions extending into Switzerland *-ena*, *-ene*, *-ën* are also found. In general the regions along the Belgian, German, and Swiss frontiers tend strongly toward monosyllabic forms. Of course many of these nasal sounds became confused in the 17th Cent., even when the nasals were followed by a vowel, $\tilde{e}$ and $\tilde{a}$ often being used interchangeably in such words as *femme*. The large number of variations is partially explained by the fact that *m* as the final element of a Latin consonant group either changed to *n* or stayed, and also by the fact that unaccented final *a* either changed to *e* or remained unchanged.[117] The short penult vowels generally dropped, though in the cases of some dialect forms there are evidences of arrested development in this as *femeno*.

[117] Hatzfeld et Darmsteter, Dict. gen. de la langue fr. 1041, and paragraphs nos. 290–1, 472, 481.

CHAPTER IX

FILLE AND FILLETTE

These and related words are derived from the Latin *filia*, the feminine of *filius*, which exists in all Romance territory.¹ The original meaning was 'suckling', but a widening of the sense was soon under way in Latin. The word gradually came to mean 'girl' and 'unmarried woman'. Even later the form came to designate the civil position of an unmarried girl in a family, possibly due to the fact that formerly the daughter of a house, when she did not get married, remained in the household of the oldest married son of her generation.² The meanings today are generally 'girl, young girl, daughter', though the common euphemistic extension to 'prostitute' is fairly frequent, and, in a few instances, the word has taken on the meaning of 'servant'.³ Among the many dialect and patois forms are the following:⁴ *fille* 2, 198, 208, 269, 334, 411, 501, 590, 600, 667,⁵ 614, 670, 989, *file* 186, 203, 284, 816, *fil*,⁶ 189, *filly* 217, *fîl*,⁷ 241, *fíl* 286,⁸ *feuille*,⁹ 380, 532,¹⁰ *fij* 435, 975,¹¹ *feille*,¹² 433, 532,¹³ 622,¹⁴ 620,¹⁵ *fiy*,¹⁶ 459, *fée* 532,¹⁷

¹ REW 3295; Kt. 3743.
² Wartburg in FEW Lief. 22.518 claims that he has found this shift in meaning attested only since the 15th Cent.
³ For the information in this paragraph see FEW Lief. 22.517-8; also Pauli, op. cit. 95-6.
⁴ Except where otherwise indicated the meanings of the following forms will be understood to be 'girl' and 'daughter'.
⁵ Pierrehumbert 667 lists this as signifying '(jeune) servante', or '(jeune) domestique'.
⁶ Pas-de-Calais, Aisne, FEW Lief. 22.516.
⁷ Ravenel (Oise), Bessin (Calvados), Manche, FEW loc. cit.
⁸ The *i* has an acute accent.
⁹ La Rochelle (Char.-Inf.), FEW loc. cit.
¹⁰ Thézey-St.-Martin (Meurthe-et-Moselle).
¹¹ Piémontais.
¹² Poitevin, FEW loc. cit.
¹³ Le Tholy (Vosges), Verdenal (Meurthe-et-Moselle), Vandéléville (Meurthe-et-Moselle), Attigny (Vosges), Gelvécourt (Vosges), Docelles (Vosges).
¹⁴ At 622 *féy* is given in parentheses after this term.
¹⁵ 'jeune fille'.
¹⁶ Western France, comprising Poitou, Anjou, Maine, H.-Bret., Normandie, FEW loc. cit.
¹⁷ Ventron (Vosges).

579, 588, 597, *feye*,[18] 532,[19] *féïe* 532,[20] 583, *fèye* 532,[21] 628,[22] *faïe* 532,[23] *fèlle* 532,[24] *fīy* 541,[25] *fey* 546, 586, 581, 589,[26] *fĭe* 553, *fœy*,[27] 560,[28] *fey*,[29] 560,[30] 622 *fēy*,[31] 560,[32] *foy* 560,[33] *feill'* 570, *féye* 579, *feye* 628,[34] *fiye* 628,[35] 760,[36] *fila* 673,[37] *fele* 682, *filhe*,[38] 682, 1094, *fiii* 702, *fàĭĕ* 703,[39] *fĕlĭĕ* 703,[40] *fĕlĭe* 703,[41] *féie* 583, *fĕy*,[42] 589, *fili* 686,[43] 687, 772, *fele* 709,[44] *file* 709,[45] *fĕle* 721,[46] *fe-ya* 751, *fil(y)i* 755, *filli*,[47] 756, 764, 767, 775, *fyele* 764,[48] *fthele* 764,[49]

[18] Vitteaux (Côte-d'Or).
[19] Hergugney Vosges).
[20] See note 13.
[21] See note 13.
[22] Vitteaux (Côte-d'Or).
[23] See note 13.
[24] See note 13.
[25] The *i* bears an acute accent directly over the long mark.
[26] Thiefosse (Vosges).
[27] Doubs, Jura, FEW loc. cit.; *œ* bears a hook directly under it opening to the right.
[28] Messin patois at Vigy (Moselle); Nied patois at Frécourt (Haute-Marne) at Sorbey (Moselle), and at Remilly (Moselle).
[29] Wallon, Lorraine, Namur (Belg.), FEW loc. cit.; *e* bears a hook directly under it opening to the right.
[30] L'Isle patois at Maizières (Meurthe-et-Moselle) and at Verny (Moselle); Pays-Haut patois at Amanvillers (Moselle) and at Gorze (Moselle); Fentsch patois at Fontoy (Moselle).
[31] Vosges patois of the Moselle, principally Réchicourt (Moselle) and Lorquin (Moselle), FEW loc. cit.
[32] Sounois patois at Dieuze (Moselle); Château-Salins (Moselle); Ommeray (Moselle).
[33] Nied (Moselle); *o* bears a hook under it opening to the right.
[34] Sancey (Meurthe-et-Moselle) and Doubs (Doubs).
[35] Mesnay (Jura).
[36] Plural.
[37] Bois d'Amont (Jura).
[38] Old Gascon, FEW loc. cit.
[39] REW 3219: *fata* 'fairy'. At Annecy (Haute-Savoie). Constantin and Désormaux 703 also give 'jeune fille éveillée'.
[40] Douvaine (Haute-Savoie) and Mûres (Haute-Savoie).
[41] Samoëns (Haute-Savoie), Conflans (Haute-Savoie), Beaufort (Savoie).
[42] The *e* bears a dot under it; Vosges méridionales, FEW loc. cit.
[43] Brütting, J., Das Bauern-Französisch in Dancourts Lustspielen, Erlangen, 1911; a short horizontal stroke turned up at right end and down at left crosses the bar of *l*.
[44] Plural; Puitspelu, 'Un conte en patois lyonnaise', Rev. de phil. fr. et de lit., 1887, 1.107–119; in source each *e* is printed as international phonetic symbol for French mute *e*.
[45] Possoz, M., 'Chanson en patois de Séez (Savoie)', Rev. de phil. fr. et de lit., 1.226–228; final *e* as in note 44.
[46] In source a tiny echo *y* is printed between *l* and final *e*.
[47] Fribourgeois (Suisse rom.); see Pauli, op. cit. 96 n2.
[48] *L* as in note 43; final *e* printed in source as in note 44; also *fel* (*l* as in note 43) at Blonay (Suisse rom.), see Pauli, op. cit.
[49] In source *th* is printed as Greek letter theta; final *e* as in note 44.

FILLE AND FILLETTE 27

figlie 779, *filho*,[50] 788, 789, 805, 915, 917, 921, 962, 967,[51] 1008, 1009, 1015, 1044, *hillo* 788, *fiho*,[52] 788, 838, 871, *fil'a* 902,[53] *filo* 902,[54] *fil'o* 902,[55] *fiyo* 949, *fiya* 949, *fyēya* 956,[56] *fia* 975,[57] *filia* 975, *fyila* 978,[58] *figlio* 987, *fielho* 988, *fillo* 990, *fede* 1020,[59] *filha*,[60] 1020, *hilha* 1020, *hilho* 1022, 1044, 1057, *hilhe* 1028, 1032, 1088, 1090, 1093, 1094, *hille* 1036, 1047, *filho* 1057, *fillas*,[61] *fëye*,[62] *filie*,[63] *fillé*,[64] *filye*,[65] *fele*,[66] *flie*,[67] *felie*,[68] *fœl*,[69] *f'lle* (*fele*),[70] *feïy*,[71] *fey*,[72] *fele*,[73] *fede*,[74] *fiyi*,[75] *feya*,[76] *filo*,[77] *fio*,[78] *hilo*,[79] *hile*,[80] *hila*,[81] *fīi*,[82] *fīa*,[83] *fila*,[84] *fíya*,[85] *fīo*.[86]

[50] Savoie; see Pauli, op. cit., 96.
[51] See note 50.
[52] Old Fribourgeois; FEW, Lief. 22.516.
[53] Old Dauph., FEW, loc. cit.
[54] Old Prov., FEW, loc. cit.; *o* bears a dot directly under it.
[55] Old Gasc., FEW loc. cit.; *o* as in note 54.
[56] Wallon, FEW, loc. cit.
[57] Lorraine, FEW, loc. cit.
[58] Namur (Belg.), FEW, loc. cit.; *l* as in note 43.
[59] Pas-de-Calais, FEW, loc. cit.
[60] Aisne, FEW, loc. cit.
[61] Ravenel (Oise), FEW, loc. cit.
[62] Bessin (Calvados), FEW, loc. cit.
[63] Manche, FEW, loc. cit.
[64] Western France, comprising Poit., Ang., Maine, H.-Bret., Norm., FEW, loc. cit.
[65] Poit., FEW, loc. cit.
[66] See note 65; *l* bears a dot directly under it.
[67] Valley of the Seudre and of the Seugne (Char.-Inf.), FEW, loc. cit.
[68] La Rochelle (Char.-Inf.), FEW, loc. cit.
[69] Saunois, patois of the region of Château-Salins and Dieuze (Moselle), FEW, loc. cit.; *l* as in note 43.
[70] Vosges patois of the Moselle, principally Réchicourt (Moselle) and Lorquin (Moselle), FEW, loc. cit.; in parenthetical form both *e*'s as in note 44, *l* as in note 43.
[71] La Baroche (Haut-Rhin), FEW, loc. cit.
[72] Vosges méridionales, FEW, loc. cit.; *e* bears a dot directly under it.
[73] Vitteaux (Côte-d'Or), FEW, loc. cit., both *e*'s as in note 44, *l* as in note 43.
[74] Doubs, FEW, loc. cit.; both *e*'s as in note 44; in source *d* is printed as Greek letter delta.
[75] Jura, FEW, loc. cit.
[76] Fribourg (in Waadt canton, Switz.), FEW, loc. cit.
[77] Monthey (in Valais canton, Switz.), FEW, loc. cit.; *l* as in note 43; Wartburg 677 contains *fede* (a dot over each *e*, dot under *d*), 'jeune servante'.
[78] Ain, FEW, loc. cit.
[79] Savoie, Haute-Savoie, FEW, loc. cit.; *l* as in note 43.
[80] Lyon, FEW, loc. cit.; *l* as in note 43.
[81] Villefranche-sur-Saône (Rhône); FEW, loc. cit.; *l* as in note 43.
[82] Grenoble (Isère), FEW, loc. cit.
[83] Languedoc, FEW, loc. cit.
[84] See note 83; *l* as in note 43.
[85] Limousin (modern dépts. of Corrèze and H.-Vienne), FEW, loc. cit.
[86] Gasc., FEW, loc. cit.

28   WORDS AND DESCRIPTIVE TERMS FOR 'WOMAN' AND 'GIRL'

On map 570, in expressions for 'ma fille', the Atlas Linguistique de la France gives many other variants. Map 1569, which records the dialect occurrences of 'fillette' in the expression 'votre fillette est-elle déjà baptisée?', gives a number of variants of 'fille'. Map 1477, 'bru', includes a very few.

The following variants of *fillette* 'young girl, little girl' were recorded by me:[87] *fillette*,[88] 198, 233, 282, *fillote* 450,[89] *fiette* 553, *feïatte* 588, *fálta* 667,[90] *filheto*,[91] 788, 789, 917, 921, *fihoto* 788, *fiéto* 788, *fuilleto* 848, *filleto*, 940, *filhèto* 1008, *hilhoto* 1022, *hilhote* 1094, *fœyat*,[92] *feyot*,[93] *feleta*,[94] *fléta*,[95] *fileta*,[96] *filett*,[97] *fileto*,[98] *fiotte*,[99] *filhoto*.[100]

A survey of terms listed in the ALF shows that *fīy* and *fēy* are the forms most common to the region along the Belgian border; *fœy, fǽl, fele*,[101] *fǽya* belong on the Swiss border; *fĭle, fĭla* are common to the Italian border; *fil, fīy* are most common in N. E. France and N. Central France; *fǽy, fūl(o), fĭl*,[102] belong to S. Central France; *hīlo, hĭlo, fīlo*,[103] are most common in the region of France near and bordering on Spain.

[87] See note 98.
[88] Val d'Aran, valley of the upper Garonne belonging to Spain but Gascon-speaking, FEW, loc. cit.
[89] Poit., FEW, loc. cit.
[90] Œ bears a hook as in note 27, *l* as in note 43.
[91] Savoie, FEW, loc. cit.
[92] Ronco Canavese (Piémont, prov. Torino), FEW, loc. cit.; Jaberg, K., and Jud, J., Sprach- und Sachatlas Italiens und der Südschweiz (AIS), Zofingen, 1928 ff., p. 132.
[93] Bruzolo (Piémont, prov. Torino), FEW, loc. cit.; see also AIS, p. 143.
[94] Pramollo (Waldenstäler in Piémont), FEW, loc. cit., see also AIS, p. 152: identical form at Sauze di Cesana (Piémont, prov. Torino), see AIS, p. 150; first *e* as in note 44, second *e* as in note 29, *l* as in note 43.
[95] Pontechianale (Piémont, prov. Cuneo), FEW, loc. cit., see also AIS, p. 160; *l* as in note 43.
[96] Pietraporzio (Piémont, prov. Cuneo), FEW, loc. cit.; see also AIS, p. 170; *l* as in note 43, *e* as in note 29.
[97] Valdieri (Piémont, prov. Cuneo), FEW, loc. cit.; see also AIS, p. 181; *l* as in note 43; *e* as in note 72.
[98] FEW Lief. 21.516–517. An O. Fr. form *fillette*, 'little girl', 'young girl', has existed since the 12th Cent. The O. Prov. form is *filheta* (rarely *filhota*). Since the 15th Cent. the Fr. form had the additional meaning of 'prostitute' in Boulogne, Dijon, and Poitiers, as did the Prov. from beginning in the same period in the region of the Basses-Alpes dépt., also Mid. Fr. *fillote*, 'little girl'. Pauli, op. cit., 95–96, observes that a number of other words mean the same thing that *fille* did originally and that, for this reason, the word *fille* has come euphemistically to mean 'prostitute' and that to express the original meaning of *fille* it is now usually necessary to have recourse to some such expression as 'jeune fille' or 'jeune personne'. *L* as in note 43, *e* as in note 72.
[99] Kt. 2751: *filiottus*, dialect form and deriv. of *filius*.
[100] Le Havre (banlieu). See FEW Lief. 22.516.
[101] In source first *e* of this form is printed with a dot directly under it, and *l* is printed bearing a tiny arc directly under it opening toward the top.
[102] *L* of this third form as in note 101.
[103] *L* of this third form as in note 101.

CHAPTER X

GAHE, GAGE, GAGUI, GAJA

There is some doubt as to the origin of such terms as *gahe, gage, gagui*, though in all probability they are related. *Gaja* 57, 'a plump woman, giddy, talkative,'[1] may be from V. L. *gajus* 'jay', or from the same root as Fr. *gai*, i.e. Frankish *wāhi* 'sparkling, pretty',[2] or the Old High German *gâhi* 'quick, nimble, sudden',[3] Littré defines *gagui* as 'a girl who is plump and lively', but says that the term is of popular origin and that the etymon is unknown.[4] These terms occur in the dialects: *gâgui* 647 'fat, dull girl, slovenly, and of little virtue'; *gágui* 703 'girl or woman of evil life';[5] *gaga* 105 'gagui, woman or girl who is plump and lively, talkative woman, flighty woman'; *gage* 419 'girl'. If one were to suppose that these terms had a common etymon which was the same as that of Fr. *gai*, the inherent semantics would seem logical. The meanings of these forms vary, and yet all the meanings could have had their origin in the different implications read into the word 'gay' itself, ranging from the respectable idea of 'cheerfulness' to 'colorfulness' and then 'gaiety' and 'promiscuity'. We have also *gahe 532* 'girl',[6] *gâhe* 532 'girl'.[7]

[1] There is no connection between this and It. *gaja*, Lat. *căvĕă* > *găvĕă* 'hollow, cavity'. See Kt. 2040.

[2] See REW 9477a. Meyer-Lübke states that Gam. is doubtful of this derivation from *gai*, because it presupposes a Fr. *jai* that has not been attested, but the former adds that the existence of Prov. *gaillard* from the same root proves that the development of *w-* to *g-* did take place under similar circumstances.

[3] Pierre-la-Treiche, Domgermain (Meurthe-et-M.), Brechainville (Vosges), Bouillonville (Meurthe-et-M.).

[4] Littré, op. cit. 2.1814.

[5] Thonon-les-Bains (H.-Savoie).

[6] Raville (Meurthe-et-M.).

[7] Martincourt (Meurthe-et-M.).

CHAPTER XI

GARCE, GACHE, GECHOTTE

A number of etyma have been suggested for this word and others on the same stem· Frank. *wurkjo[1] or *wrakjo[2] 'worker', *cardeo (< carduus 'thistle'),[3] Germ. *wartja[4] 'anything that grows from the earth, root'. Possibly there is a connection with the Irish gearsa-orca 'a lazy fat woman'[5] and garcionem.[6] Garçon, the masc. and more common form, is attested in the 12th Cent. Chanson de Roland. Métivier has suggested Irish cognates geirleach 'boy' and geirsheag, geirsheog 'young girl'.[7] The Frank. personal name Wracchio of the 9th Cent. is attested and is similar to Old Saxon wrekko, Old High Germ. rekko 'a banished person, warrior in the pay of foreigners', Old Eng. wrecca 'rascal'.[8] Fr. garçonnet of the 13th Cent. and garconnière of the 12th Cent. 'one who likes to play with garcons' are given by Bloch.[9] Garce, a 13th Cent. form, then meant 'young girl', but in the 16th Cent. took on a pejorative meaning; the Mod. Fr. usage is still pejorative—'woman of the town, loose person'.[10] Garcette, a 13th Cent. dim., has not been used in its proper sense since the 16th Cent.[11] There are quite a number of dialect and patois forms that we have recorded: garce 57 'fille débauchée'; garss 105 'prostituée, fille de joie'; gârce

---

[1] REW 9578a. Fuller's commentary is worthy of note: '. . . as also Bartholomew de Walton, and William his brother, because waited on by William de Merton, their garcion, that is "their servant". For it cometh from the French garçon, or the Italian garzone and is a word even used by the barbarous Grecians of the Middle Ages.' Fuller, Hist. of Cambridge and of Waltham Abbey, London, 1840, p. 24, citing Scholiastis Cendrini. Malzevin makes the statement that gars '. . . égale à bars et à vars, éminence'.—P. Malzevin, Dict. des racines celtiques (2nd ed.). Paris, 1924, p. 80. Also see G. G. Nicholson, Rev. de ling. rom., 5.64–5, < *wartio; Idem., Romania 50.98 < *wartione.

[2] Bloch 1.327.

[3] Diez 2c.

[4] Kt. 10360.

[5] P. S. Dineen, An Irish-English Dict., Dublin, 1927, p. 146.

[6] Pauli cites the accepted theory that garçon is derived from V. L. *garcionem and that it is the objective case of gars, but his own less probable theory is that garçon is derived from the Medieval gars plus the suffix -on. -Ivan Pauli, 'Enfant', 'Garcon', 'Fille' dans les langues romanes, Lund, 1919, pp. 151 ff.

[7] See Métivier, Dict. franco-norm., London and Edinburg, 1870.

[8] See note 2.

[9] See note 2.

[10] See note 2.

[11] See note 2.

150 'evil woman'; *gáars* 182 'prostitute'; *garce* 214 'prostitute; *garsonnière* 214 'loose girl who imitates or likes boys too much'; *garchonnière* 233; *garce* 284 'virgin, young girl'; *garsounière* 284 'girl who likes boys too much';[12] *garce* 357; *garce* 398 'young girl';[13] *garse* 398 'young girl';[14] *gairse* 468 'girl'; *gairse* 478 'girl';[15] *garcelle* 478 'young girl';[16] *garce* 522 'girl';[17] *gas* 546 'girl'; *garse* 632 'little girl'; *garce* 640 'prostitute'; *guerça* 647 'prostitute'; *garça* 647 'prostitute'; *garça* 715 'prostitute'; *garci* 759 'femme débauchée, mauvaise personne'; *guerci* 759 'femme débauchée, mauvaise personne';[18] *garçonaille* 748 'femme fort dépréciant, fille à garçons'; *garco* 786 'young girl, prostitute'; *garso* 788 'prostitute';[19] *garseto* 788 'young girl';[20] *garsounièro* 788 'young girl who frequents boys and has their tastes and manners'; *garsa* 959 'mistress of the household'; *garso* 970 'girl of evil life who likes boys'; *garso* 980 'girl'; *garso* 1023 'young girl'.[21]

ALF 570 'fille' includes the following: n336 *gărsĕt* (Orne);[22] n471 *gārs* (Côtes-du-N.);[23] n709 *gărsŭnĕl* (Cantal);[24] n399 *gārs* (Guernesey);[25] n396 *gārs* (Aurigny).

Gache and *gechotte* are of the same origin as *garse*, etc., though the consonant *r* has disappeared, the vowel-plus-*r*-plus-dental-sibilant combination having become in most cases a vowel-plus-palatal-sibilant. There has also been in some cases a notable influence from forms *bacelle*, etc.[26] The usual meaning is that of 'girl': *gâche* 532,[27] *gache* 532,[28] *gäx* 560,[29]

---

[12] Métivier also cites Valogne *garsonniere*, of the same meaning.
[13] Not always in a pejorative sense.
[14] Always pejoratively.
[15] Ardennes.
[16] See note 15.
[17] Slightly pejorative.
[18] A Celt. *garchain* 'prostituée' is given as an etymon.
[19] Formerly 'young girl'.
[20] Pejoratively; also *garsoto* with same meaning.
[21] Often taken pejoratively. Durrieux refers to Gr. ἄρσην and to Celt. *gwaz, ar, gur*.
[22] *A* bears an almost vertical stroke under it extending from bottom of letter toward lower left.
[23] Becoming obsolete.
[24] In source a tiny italic type *a* bearing a grave accent follows *l*.
[25] See note 23.
[26] See chapter XXVI.
[27] Pierre-laTreiche, Domgermain (Meurthe-et-M.), Brechainville (Vosges), Bouillonville (Meurthe-et-M.).
[28] See note 2.
[29] Messin pat. at Vigy; Nied pat. at Frécourt, Sorbey, and Rémilly; *a* bears a long mark directly above the diaeresis.

gāx 560,³⁰ *gās* 560,³¹ *gōs* 560,³² *gaswt* 604 'petite fille', *gesat* 608, *gechotte* 623, *ghèchòte* 628 'jeune fille', *gaichotte* 647 'jeune fille'.³³

The ALF map 570 'fille' lists variants of *gache* and *gechotte* under numbers 4, 26, 27, 28, 38, 47, 48, 54, 110, 121, 153, 154, 163, 164, 173, 901. These are in the Nièvre, Haute-Saône, Haute-Marne, Vosges, Doubs, Meuse, Meurthe-et-M. departments. There is one occurrence in Allier and another in Côte-d'Or.

[30] L'Isle pat. at Maizières and Verny; Pays-Haut pat. at Amanvillers and Gorze.
[31] Fentsch pat. at Fontoy; *s* bears a long mark directly over it.
[32] See note 6; *s* bears a short mark directly over it.
[33] Evêche de Bâle; *baichotte* also occurs here—a witness to the fact of influence of *gas* on *basse*, etc.; in support of this see also ALF 570: n74 *bēcot* (*e* bearing grave accent directly above long mark, and a short straight stroke starting in middle of *c* loop and crossing arc toward left and bottom), and n54 *gĕcōt* (each vowel bearing a grave accent in addition, and *c* as above).

Chapter XII

GORE

The probable etymon of this word is that given by Meyer-Lübke, *gorr* 'onomatopoeic word for calling pigs', appearing in O. Fr. as written above, as *gorre*, Poitev. *gor* 'sow, hog'; Forez *gurina* 'maid, girl, low woman'; and a number of masc. forms.[1] Schuchardt's derivation of it from Celt. *goiros, Greek χοῖρος 'pig', is unlikely.[2] Diez's derivation from Germ. *gorren* 'to grunt' is more feasible than the former, though the semantic possibilities of the first etymon suggested are more within the realm of reason than either of the others.[3] One can readily understand how a command word could take on the characteristics of an uncomplimentary epithet and then become generalized as a noun with pejorative connotations. Dialect and patois occurrences are: *gore* 217, *gore* 309,[4] *gorillette* 309,[5] *gore* 373,[6] *gore* 398,[7] *gora* 759,[8] *gourrinasso* 789 'femme impudique', *gourrino* 789 'prostituée',[9] *goro* 814, *gourrino* 828 'femme de mauvaise vie', *gorra* 959, *gorro*, *gourra* 959, *gourro* 959, *giora* 975,[10] *gora*[11] 975.[12]

[1] REW 3820: *gorron, gorrel,* masc. 'pig', in O. Fr.; *goret* 'pig' in Mod. Fr. Gam. 476: there are also quite a number of fem. dialect forms where meanings other than 'sow' are not attested.

[2] Schuchardt, ZRP, 30.213.

[3] Diez, 601.

[4] Esnault remarks that the *gorillette* is more lively and the *gore* more professional, that the root is *gore* 'sow with little pigs' used in Vannes, 1744, and that the word seems to have come to Basse-Bretagne from below the Loire.

[5] See note 4.

[6] Jônain cites in this connection the Eng. *whore*.

[7] Jaubert gives the meaning 'sow, fig. dissolute woman'. *Goure* also appears in this Glos. du Centre, but with only the meaning of the fem. of *goret*, i.e. 'sow'.

[8] Duplay gives the meanings 'sow, old cow; fig. woman of evil life' and cites Celt. *goria*.

[9] In Rouergue this means 'sorcière'.

[10] Piémontais.

[11] Auvergnat.

[12] See further: Tappolet in Herrigs Archiv 131.111; Nigra in Archivio glottologico italiano 15.144.

CHAPTER XIII

GOUGE

This was borrowed from the southern French *gouja* 'servant girl', from the Hebrew *goja* 'maid servant'.[1] This etymology is accepted by a number of the authorities,[2] thought Bloch claims that the word is of obscure origin.[3] Godefroy lists a masculine form of the same spelling, which is attested in 1337, and a feminine form, *gougie* 'servant girl'.[4] The word is used to mean 'woman' or 'girl' in a very familiar, and often a disparaging sense.[5] It is attested in the 15th Cent.[6] The modern French meaning is either that of 'maid-servant', without any pejorative connotation, or vulgarly 'woman'.[7] Cotgrave defines *gouge* 'a whore who follows the camp', and *goujate* 'a souldier's wench'.[8] Among its occurrences are: *gougouie* 57 'woman who loves good cheer', *goujarde* 226 'femme a soldats', *gouge* 398 'woman of evil life',[9] *goyote* 453 'poorly clothed woman', *gouge* 522 'prostitute', *goujate* 783 'servant', *goujo* 786 'servant', 'shepherdess', 'mountain girl', *goujouleto* 786 'little girl', 'pet servant',[10] *goujatero* 786[11] 'young girl who runs after young men', *goujo* 789[12] 'servant', *goujardo* 789[13] 'girl', 'fiancée', *goujardasso* 789[14] 'fat girl', *goujeto* 789 'pet girl', 'maid', *gouxo* 921 'fille', *gougio* 921 'fille', *gouyate* 1020 'fille', *gouye* 1020 'fille', *goujato* 1023 'young girl', *goujatto* 1023[15] 'young girl', *goujouleto* 1023 'young girl', *gouyate* 1032 'young girl', *gouyate* 1035 'young girl', *guye* 1036 'young girl',[16] *gouyato* 1044 'young girl', *gouiato* 1045 'young girl', *gouio* 1045 'young girl', 'servant', *goujate* 1088 'young girl', *gouge* 1088 'maid servant',

[1] REW 3818c.
[2] Diez 601, REW 3818c, Gam. 478, Pauli 349, Kt. 4295. Diez says it is the Heb. *goje* 'Christian servant'.
[3] Bloch 1.342.
[4] Godefroy 4.317.
[5] Littré 2.1897.
[6] See note 5.
[7] Clifton and Grimaux, A New French-English Dict., Paris, 1923, p. 659.
[8] Cotgrave, op. cit., see *gouge*.
[9] Jaubert remarks that the Academy mentions only *gouge* 'laborer's chisel', which is derived from Latin *gubia* 'chisel'. See REW 3906.
[10] Gascon.
[11] Béarnais.
[12] In Languedoc and Gascony.
[13] Guienne.
[14] Querdy.
[15] Durrieux proposes an untenable Greek etymon ἄζυγος, *ἀζύγωτος. 'who has not yet been put under the yoke'.
[16] At Sabres.

gouyate 1090 'young girl', *gouyate* 1093 'girl', *gouyatine* 1093 'little girl', *gouye* 1093 'maid servant', *goutote* 1093 'little maid servant', *gouge* 1094 'unmarried girl or woman',[17] *gouye* 1094, *goge* 1094, *gouyate* 1094 'girl', *gouyatere* 'fille qui fréquente les garçons', *gouyate* 1100 'girl', *gouyatote* 1100 'young girl', *gouye* 1100 'maid servant'.

ALF map 1226 'servante' includes variants of this word in numbers 634, 635, 637, 645, 647, 648, 656, 657, 658, 664, 665, 668, 669, 672, 676, 678, 681, 685, 688, 689, 691, 692, 693, 694, 695, 696, 697, 731, 741, in the departments of Gironde, Lot-et-Garonne, Gers, Landes, Basses-Pyrénées, Hautes-Pyrénées, and Tarn-et-Garonne. On map 570 'fille' forms of *gouge* are under numbers 641, 643, 645, 658, 675, 681, 683, 684, 548, 549, for Gironde, Gers, and Landes.

[17] The two terms following have the same meaning as this.

CHAPTER XIV

GOUINE

An accepted etymology for this word is yet to be found, though several have been proposed. Diez connected it with *godine* and *godinette*, 'gay, merry girl', as a derivative from the root *gaud-*: Lat. *gaudere*, 'to rejoice', 'make merry';[1] but he condemned such an etymon as Eng. *quean*, 'woman of evil life', related to Anglo-Saxon *cwen* and to Icelandic *quinna*, 'woman'.[2] Creuzé de Lesser in his poem *La Table Ronde*, chant VI, derives this word from Queen *Goïne*, who deceived her husband and made him perish in order to elope with her lover.[2] Körting suggests the Celtic stem *got-*, Old Irish *gothimm*, Welsh *godinet*, meaning 'prostitution', from which he also derives Modern Prov. *goda*, 'foul wench', 'hussy', Old Fr. *godon*, as well as *gouine*.[3] The latter three have the same meaning. It would seem, as Littré suggests, that the Icelandic form is most apt to be the correct etymology. Neither Gamillscheg nor Meyer-Lübke commits himself concerning this word. Among its occurrences in the dialects and patois are: *gouine* 226, *gouyne* 226, *gouine* 233,[4] *gouine* 356, *gouine* 373, *gouine* 398, *gouine* 426,[5] *gouingne* 453, *gouine* 486, *gouine* 522, *gwină* 703,[6] *guïnă* 715,[8] *gouine* 748, *gourina* 759, *goino* 786, *gouïno* 786, *goyno* 786,[9] *gouino* 789,[10] *gouino* 789,[11] *guino* 789,[12] *goueino* 789,[12] *goino* 789,[13] *goueno* 806, *gouina* 810, 'woman wearing immodest clothes', *gouineou* 810, 'bady dressed woman', *gouinella* 810, 'badly dressed woman', *gouinilla* 810, 'woman of ungraceful bearing, overdressed', *goueïno* 987, *gu-ïno* 991. The meaning of the term in Modern Fr. and except where otherwise stated is that of 'prostitute', or 'street walker'. In the Provençal regions it is used as an adjective and as a substantive.

[1] Diez, 599.
[2] Littré, op. cit. 2. 1898.
[3] Kt, 4302.
[4] Maze suggests a connection with Greek γυνή, which is cognate with 'queen', etc.
[5] Mignard says the English borrowed this word from the Burgundians, their allies under Philippe-le-Bon in the 15th Cent. He states that it was pronounced [kouine], written *quean*, and meant 'tramp', or 'vagabond'.
[6] At Albertville.
[7] At Lyon.
[8] 'Femme vêtue de guenilles'.
[9] Boucoiran suggests a connection with Greek κοινός, 'common'.
[10] Gascon.
[11] Limousin.
[12] Dauphinois.
[13] Rougerat, has the meaning of 'sorceress' and 'fairy' here, as well as the usual one.